THE PEN

OF

SOLOMON

S. Aldarnay

THE PENTANCLES OF SOLOMON

Hadean Press
France

ISBN 978 1 907881 22 0

AUTHOR'S NOTE: Text in quotation marks is taken from *The Key
of Solomon the King (Clavicular Salomonis)*, translated & edited by
S Liddell MacGregor Mathers in 1888. I have left this text as it
stands so that people can infer what they will from the description
of the pentacles' usage.

THE PENTACLES

OF

SOLOMON

S. ALDARNAY

INTRODUCTION
by S. Aldarnay

THE PENTACLES OF SOLOMON HAVE LONG BEEN A SOURCE OF INSPIRATION, NOT just for ceremonial magicians, but to all manner of students of the occult. However, in this modern day and age where study of Hebrew and Latin has become a less important aspect of magical training, many people are confused or just ignorant of the greater meanings behind these magical images, taking them as merely arcane symbols, and putting all their faith in the authors of the numerous books on the subject rather than the actual powers at work behind each seal. Here I have attempted to render the pentacles in a clear and concise fashion, allowing even the casual practitioner to begin to understand some of the underlying source of the pentacles' power, primarily the psalms and divine names present in their designs. Whilst it is true to say that the pentacles of Solomon are a diverse magical tool, their design is highly dependent on the use of the Kabbalistic names of God, angels and spirits as well as the vesicles (the text running around the outer edge of most pentacles) which are taken from the *Book of Psalms* or various texts from the Old Testament.

The pentacles I have chosen to examine are taken from the Mather's edition of the *Key of Solomon*, as I believe that these are the most widely recognised, and utilised, of the myriad images called Pentacles of Solomon. However, these are also some of the most badly rendered images available. This is no one's fault *per se*, but it does make reproduction of the pentacles very difficult, and as previously mentioned, many people have little to no knowledge of the Hebrew language and as such vitally important words are often misspelled or devolve into meaningless scribbles. In the following pages I have presented each of the Pentacles given in the *Key of Solomon*, redrawn and with explanations of the divine names, the names of spirits, as well as the vesicles in English, Latin and Hebrew, in an attempt to make the individual's use of the seals more effective.

Whilst I am by no means an expert in this field of magic, I hope that this text will be beneficial to beginners as well as those who are accustomed to the magic of the pentacles. By presenting the pentacles in full I hope that people will be inclined to experiment more with them as, in my opinion, they are able to bridge the gap between the high magic of angelic conjuration and divine names, and the folk magic which utilizes psalms and spiritual assistance for more day to day concerns.

THE MYSTICAL FIGURE OF SOLOMON

SUGGESTED CIRCLE FOR CONSECRATING PENTACLES

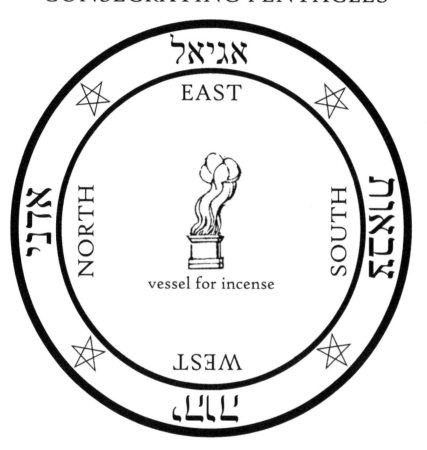

אגיאל

EAST

NORTH

SOUTH

אדני

צבאות

vessel for incense

WEST

יהוי

Divine Names

East: Agiel   South: Tzabaoth

North:Adonai   West:IHVI

PENTACLES OF SATURN

1 - Stirkes terror into spirits
2- Against adversities and the pride of
spirits
3- For invoking spirits of Saturn by
night
4- For destruction and ruin, also for the
conjuratoin of messenger spirits
5- Defends those who conjure spirits,
and chases away treasure spirits
6- To instigate demonic attack
7-to cause earthquakes

These pentacles should be made on a
Saturday, from lead or on virgin
parchment using black ink.

FIRST PENTACLE OF
SATURN

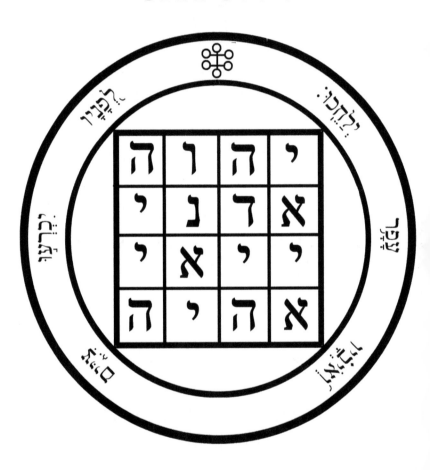

"This Pentacle is of great value and utility for striking terror into the Spirits. Wherefore, upon its being shown to them they submit, and kneeling upon the earth before it, they obey."

The central square contains the following divine names:
IHVH, Yod, He, Vau, He
ADNI - Adonai
IIAI - Yiai
AHIH - Eheieh
The versicle is psalm 72:9:
They that dwell in the wilderness shall bow before him; And his enemies shall lick the dust.

Posuerunt in caelum os suum et lingua eorum transivit in terra

וְאֹיְבָיו צִיִּים יִכְרְעוּ לְפָנָיו

יְלַחֵכוּ: עָפָר

SECOND PENTACLE OF SATURN

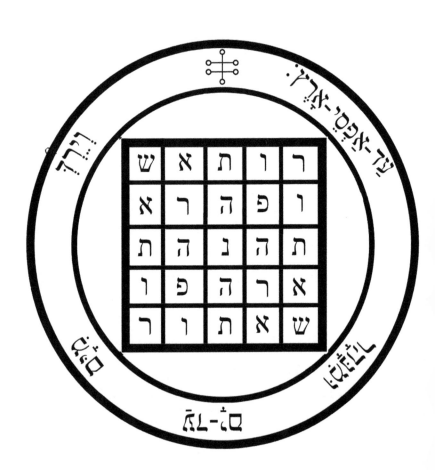

"This Pentacle is of great value against adversities; and of especial use in repressing the pride of the Spirits."

S	A	T	O	R
A	R	E	P	O
T	E	N	E	T
O	P	E	R	A
R	O	T	A	S

The central square here contains the famous "Sator" double acrostic, which is reputed to have many occult virtues.

The vericle of this pentacle is Psalm 72:8

'His dominion shall be also from the one sea to the other, and from the flood unto the world's end"

Et dominabitur a mari usque ad mare et a flumine usque ad terminos orbis terrarum

וְיֵרְדְּ, מִיָּם עַד-יָם;וּמִנָּהָר, עַד- אַפְסֵי-אָרֶץ.

THIRD PENTACLE OF SATURN

"This should be made within the Magical Circle, and it is good for use at night when thou invokest the Spirits of the nature of Saturn."

The symbols around the spokes at the centre of the pentacle are mystical characters of Saturn.

The four hebrew words surrounding the pentacle are the names of the following angels:

Omeliel	עמליאל:
Anachiel	אנחיאל:
Arauchiah	ארוכיה:
Anazachiav	אנצחיה:

FOURTH PENTACLE OF SATURN

"This Pentacle serveth principally for executing all the experiments and operations of ruin, destruction, and death. And when it is made in full perfection, it serveth also for those Spirits which bring news, when thou invokest them from the side of the South."

The text around the triangle is Deuterronomy 6:4:
Hear, O Israel: the LORD our GOD, the LORD is one. Hear, O Israel, IHVH ALHINV is IHVH AChD.

The versicle here is Psalm 109:18
As he clothed himself with cursing like as with a garment, so let it come into his bowels like water, and like oil into his bones
Et induit maledictionem sicut vestimentum et intravit sicut aqua in interiora eius et sicut oleum in ossibus eius.

וַיִּלְבַּשׁ קְלָלָה,כְּמַדּוֹ:וַתָּבֹא כַמַּיִם בְּקִרְבּוֹ;וְכַשֶּׁמֶן,בְּעַצְמוֹתָיו

FIFTH PENTACLE OF SATURN

"This Pentacle defendeth those who invoke the Spirits of Saturn during the night; and chaseth away the Spirits which guard treasures."

DIVINE NAMES
יהוה IHVH
אלוה ALVH - Eloah

ANGELIC NAMES
ארהנה: Arehanah
רכניאל: Rakhaniel
רואלהיפר: Roelhaiphar
נואפיאל: Noaphiel.

The versicle here is Deuteronomy 10:17

A Great God, Mighty, and Terrible

Deus magnus et potens, et terribilis

הָאֵל הַגָּדֹל הַגִּבֹּר וְהַנּוֹרָא

SIXTH PENTACLE OF SATURN

"*Around this Pentacle is each Name symbolised as it should be. The person against whom thou shalt pronounce it shall be obsessed by Demons.*"

The symbols radiating form the central arms are mystical characters of saturn.

The versicle is Psalm 109:6:

"*Set thou a wicked one to be ruler over him, and let Satan stand at his right hand.*"

Constitue super eum impium et Satan astet a dextris eius

הַפְקֵד עָלָיו רָשָׁע וְשָׂטָן יַעֲמֹד עַל־יְמִינוֹ

SEVENTH PENTACLE
OF SATURN

"This Pentacle is fit for exciting earthquakes, seeing that the power of each order of Angels herein invoked is sufficient to make the whole Universe tremble."

The text inside the pentacle are the names of the 9 orders of angels.

1. CHAIOTH HA-QADESCH, Holy Living Creatures
2. AUPHANIM, Wheels
3. ARALIM, Thrones
4. CHASCHMALIM, Brilliant Ones
5. SERAPHIM, Fiery Ones
6. MELAKIM, Kings
7. ELOHIM, Gods
8. BENI ELOHIM, Sons of the Elohim
9. KERUBIM, Kerubim.

The versicle for this pentacle is Psalm 18:8 *'Then the earth shook and trembled, the foundations of the hills also moved and were shaken, because He was wroth.'*

Et commota est et contremuit terra et fundamenta montium conturbata sunt et commota sunt quoniam iratus est eis

וַתִּגְעַשׁ וַתִּרְעַשׁ,הָאָרֶץ-- וּמוֹסְדֵי הָרִים יִרְגָּזוּ;

וַיִּתְגָּעֲשׁוּ, כִּי-חָרָה לוֹ.

PENTACLES OF JUPITER

4

1 - For invoking the spirits of jupiter
and aquiring wealth
2 - For glory and riches
3 - Protects against summoned spirits
and causes obedience in them
4 - For wealth
5 - For Visions
6 - Against earthly danger
7 - Against Poverty

These pentacles should be made on a
Thursday from Tin, or on virgin parchment using blue ink.

FIRST PENTACLE OF JUPITER

"This serveth to invoke the Spirits of Jupiter, and especially those whose Names are written around the Pentacle, among whom Parasiel is the Lord and Master of Treasures, and teacheth how to become possessor of places wherein they are."

The characters around the spokes of this pentagram are mystical symbols of Jupiter, and the names in the versicle are those of the angels:

נתוניאל:	NETONIEL
פרסיאל:	PARASIEL
צדקיה:	TZEDEQIAH
דוחיה:	DEVACHIAH

SECOND PENTACLE OF JUPITER

-"This is proper for acquiring glory, honours, dignities, riches, and all kinds of good, together with great tranquillity of mind; also to discover Treasures and chase away the Spirits who preside over them. It should be written upon virgin paper or parchment, with the pen of the swallow and the blood of the screech-owl."

Divine Names: AHIH, AB & IHVH

The Versicle here is a version of
Psalm 112:3
"Wealth and riches are in his house; and his merit endureth for ever."

Gloria et divitiae in domo eius et iustitia eius manet in saeculum saeculi

הוֹן - וָעֹשֶׁר בְּבֵיתוֹ וְצִדְקָתוֹ עֹמֶדֶת לָעַד:

THIRD PENTACLE OF JUPITER

"This defenth and protecteth those who invoke and cause the spirits to come. when they appear show unto them this Pentacle and immediately they will obey."

Divine Names: ADONAI & IHVH

The versicle here is Psalm 125:1

They that trust in the LORD are as mount Zion, which cannot be moved, but abideth for ever.

Qui confidunt in Domino sicut mons Sion non commovebitur in aeternum qui habitat

שִׁיר, הַמַּעֲלוֹת:

הַבֹּטְחִים בַּיהוָה -- כְּהַר- צִיּוֹן לֹא--יִמּוֹט,לְעוֹלָם יֵשֵׁב:

FOURTH PENTACLE
OF JUPITER

"It serveth to acquire riches and honour, and to possess much wealth. Its Angel is Bariel. It should be engraved upon silver in the day and hour of Jupiter when he is in the Sign Cancer."

DIVINE NAME: IH - Iah
ANGELIC NAMES: Adoniel
Bariel

The Versicle here is a version of
Psalm 112:3
"Wealth and riches are in his house; and his merit endureth for ever."

Gloria et divitiae in domo eius et iustitia eius manet in saeculum saeculi

הוֹן - וָעֹשֶׁר בְּבֵיתוֹ וְצִדְקָתוֹ עֹמֶדֶת לָעַד׃

FIFTH PENTACLE OF JUPITER

"This hath great power. It serveth for assured visions. Jacob being armed with this Pentacle beheld the ladder which reached unto heaven."

The versicle is taken from Ezekiel 1:1

" *As I was among the captives by the river of Chebar, the heavens were opened, and I saw visions of Elohim.*"

cum essem in medio captivorum iuxta fluvium Chobar, aperti sunt cæli, et vidi visiones Dei.

וַאֲנִי בְתוֹךְ- הַגּוֹלָה עַל- נְהַר כְּבָר

נִפְתְּחוּ הַשָּׁמַיִם וָאֶרְאֶה מַרְאוֹת אֱלֹהִים

SIXTH PENTACLE
OF JUPITER

"It serveth for protection against all earthly dangers, by regarding it each day devoutedly, and repeating the versicle which surroundeth it. Thus shalt thou never perish."

The central cross bears the names of the rulers of the elements:
Seraph (north)
Kerub (west)
Ariel (south)
Tharsis (east)

The versicle is psalm 22:16/17
"They pierced my hands and my feet. I may tell all my bones"

Foderunt manus meas et pedes meos: dinumeraverunt omnia ossa mea

כָּאֲרִי יָדַי וְרַגְלָי ,אֲסַפֵּר כָּל-עַצְמוֹתָי

SEVENTH PENTACLE
OF JUPITER

"It hath great power against poverty, if thou considerest it with devotion, repeating the versicle. It serveth furthermore to drive away those Spirits who guard treasures, and to discover the same."

The versicle is Psalm 113:7 *"Who raiseth up the poor out of the dust, and lifteth up the needy out of the dunghill"*
Suscitans a terra inopem et de stercore erigens pauperem

מְקִימִי מֵעָפָר דָּל מֵאַשְׁפֹּת יָרִים אֶבְיוֹן

PENTACLES OF MARS

1 = For invoking the spirits of Mars
2 - Against disease of the body
3 - Causes war and discord
4 - Gives victory in war
5 - Is terrible unto demons
6 - To be unharmed by weapons, and to cause weapons to turn on thier users.
7 - To cause hail and tempests.

Make these pentacles our of iron, on a Tuesday. They can also be made using red ink on virgin parchement.

FIRST PENTACLE OF
MARS

"It is proper for invoking Spirits of the Nature of Mars, especially those which are written in the Pentacle."

Angelic Names

מאדימיאל:	MADIMIEL
אתאוריאל:	ITHURIEL
ברצחיה:	BARTZACHIAH
אשיאל:	ESCHIEL

SECOND PENTACLE OF MARS

"This Pentacle serveth with great success against all kinds of diseases, if it be applied unto the afflicted part."

DIVINE NAMES:
IHVH
IHSHVH
ELOHIM

The versicle of this pentacle is John 1:4

"*In Him was life, and the life was the light of man*"

in ipso vita erat et vita erat lux hominum

בּוֹ הָיוּ חַיִּים וְהַחַיִּים הָיוּ אוֹר לִבְנֵי הָאָדָם׃

THIRD PENTACLE OF MARS

"It is of great value for exciting war, wrath, discord, and hostility; also for resisting enemies, and striking terror into rebellious Spirits; the Names of God the All Powerful are therein expressly marked."

DIVINE NAMES
SHADDAI
ELOAH

The versicle is from Psalm 76:14

"Who is so great a God as our Elohim?"

quis deus magnus sicut Deus noster

מִי-אֵל גָּדוֹל כֵּאלֹהִים

FOURTH PENTACLE OF MARS

"It is of great virtue and power in war, wherefore without doubt it will give thee victory."

DIVINE NAMES:
EL
AGLA
IHVH

The versicle is Psalm 110:5
"The Lord at thy right hand hath broken kings in the day of his wrath."

Dominus a dextris tuis confregit in die irae suae reges

אֲדֹנָי עַל-יְמִינְךָ; מָחַץ בְּיוֹם-אַפּוֹ מְלָכִים.

FIFTH PENTACLE OF MARS

"Write thou this Pentacle upon virgin parchment or paper, because it is terrible unto the Demons, and at its sight and aspect they will obey thee, for they cannot resist its presence."

Around the central scorpion is the word: HVL

The versicle is from 91:13

"Thou shalt walk upon the asp and the basilisk: and thou shalt trample under foot the lion and the dragon."

Super aspidem et basiliscum ambulabis et conculcabis leonem et draconem

עַל-שַׁחַל וָפֶתֶן תִּדְרֹךְ; תִּרְמֹס כְּפִיר וְתַנִּין.

SIXTH PENTACLE OF MARS

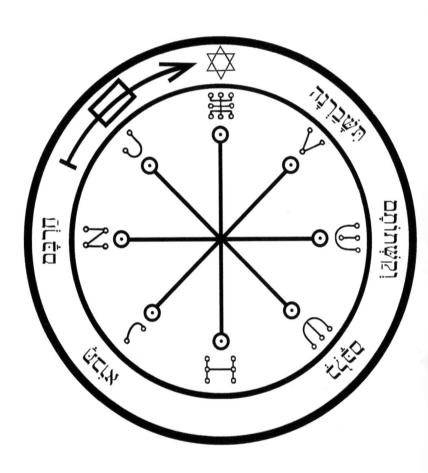

"It hath so great virtue that being armed therewith, if thou art attacked by any one, thou shalt neither be injured nor wounded when thou fightest with him, and his own weapons shall turn against him."

The symbols surrounding the 8 arms at the centre of this pentacle spell out:
ELOHIM QEBER
Elohim hath covered/protected

The versicle is Psalm 37:15
"Their sword shall enter into their own heart, and their bows shall be broken."

Gladius eorum intret in corda ipsorum et arcus ipsorum confringatur

חַרְבָּם, תָּבוֹא בְלִבָּם; וְקַשְּׁתוֹתָם, תִּשָּׁבַרְנָה.

SEVENTH PENTACLE
OF MARS

"Write thou this upon virgin parchment or paper with the blood of a bat, in the day and hour of Mars; and uncover it within the Circle, invoking the Demons whose Names are therein written; and thou shalt immediately see hail and tempest."

DIVINE NAMES: EL & YIAI

The Versicle here is Psalm 105: 32/33
"He gave them hail for rain, and flaming fire in their land. He smote their vines also, and their fig-trees"

Posuit pluvias eorum grandinem ignem conburentem in terra ipsorum
Et percussit vineas eorum et ficulneas eorum et contrivit lignum finium eorum

נָתַן גִּשְׁמֵיהֶם בָּרָד אֵשׁ לֶהָבוֹת בְּאַרְצָם וַיַּךְ גַּפְנָם

PENTACLES OF THE SUN

1 - Causes reverence in angelic spirits
2 - To Repress the pride of solar spirits
3 -For the acquisition of kingdom, empire, renown & glory
4 - To see spirits and make them manifest visibly
5 - To Invoke spirits of travel
6 - For invisiblilty
7 -For Freedom from bondage or restraint.

These pentacles should be made on a Sunday, from gold, or inscribed on virgin parchment using yellow or gold ink.

FIRST PENTACLE OF
THE SUN

"The Countenance of Shaddaï the Almighty, at Whose aspect all creatures obey, and the Angelic Spirits do reverence on bended knees."

Divine Names: Shaddai

The face is either given to be that of Shaddai himself, or the angel Metatron.

The versicle is written in latin, saying: "*Ecce faciem et figuram ejus per quem omnia faceta et cui omnes obediunt creature*"

which roughly translates to:

'Behold His face and form by Whom all things were made, and Whom all creatures obey.'

SECOND PENTACLE
OF THE SUN

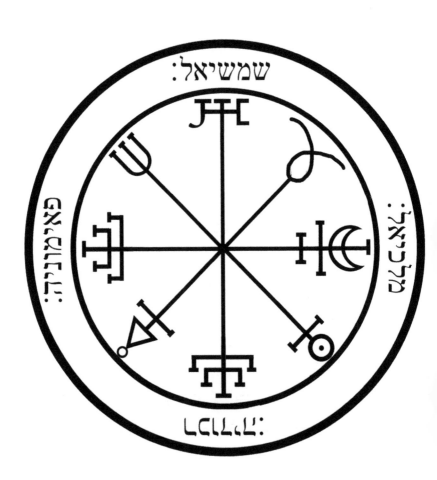

"This Pentacle, and the preceeding and following, belong to the nature of the Sun. They serve to repress the pride and arrogance of the Solar Spirits, which are altogether proud and arrogant by thier nature"

The angelic names which surround this pentacle are:

מלכיאל: Malkhiel

פאימוניה: Paimoniah

שמשיאל: Shemeshiel

רכודיה: Rekhodiah

THIRD PENTACLE OF
THE SUN

This serveth in addition (to the effects of the two preceding) to acquire Kingdom and Empire, to inflict loss, and to acquire renown and glory, especially through the Name of God, Tetragrammaton, which therein is twelve times contained.

The versicle is a variant of Daniel 4:34 'My Kingdom is an everlasting Kingdom, and my dominion endureth from age unto age.'

שָׁלְטָנֵי שָׁלְטָנֵן עָלַם וְמַלְכוּתִי עִמָדָרי וְדָר

The divine name IHVH (יהוה)is repeated 12 times within this pentacle.

FOURTH PENTACLE
OF THE SUN

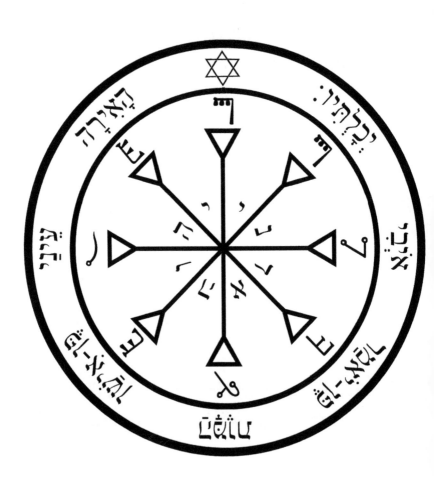

"This serveth to enable thee to see the spirits when they appear invisible unto those who invoke them; because, when thou hast uncovered it, they wwill immediately appear visible."

Divine Names: IHVH & Adonai

The vericle here is Psalm 13:4&5
"Lighten mine eyes, lest i sleep in death; Lest mine enemy say: 'I have prevailed against him"

Inlumina oculos meos ne umquam obdormiam in mortem Nequando dicat inimicus meus praevalui adversus eum

הָאִירָה עֵינַי פֶּן-אִישַׁן הַמָּוֶת
פֶּן-יֹאמַר אֹיְבִי יְכָלְתִּיו:

FIFTH PENTACLE OF THE SUN

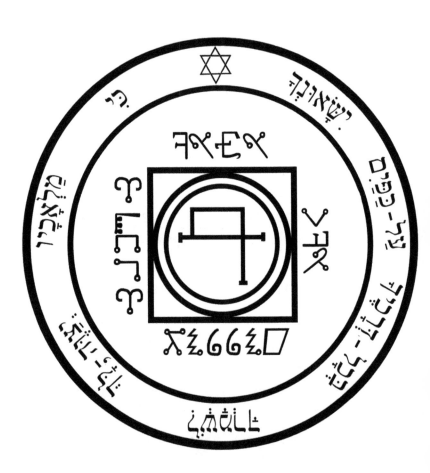

"It serveth to invoke those Spirits who can transport thee from one place unto another, over a long distance and in short time."

The characters around the central circle are from the passing the river script.

The versicle is Psalm 91:11,12
"*He shall give his angels charge over thee, to keep theee in all they ways. They shall bear thee up in a their hands*"

Quoniam angelis suis mandabit de te ut custodiant te in omnibus viis tuis In manibus portabunt te.

כִּי מַלְאָכָיו, יְצַוֶּה-לָּךְ; לִשְׁמָרְךָ, בְּכָל-דְּרָכֶיךָ

עַל — כַּפַּיִם יִשָּׂאוּנְךָ

SIXTH PENTACLE OF THE SUN

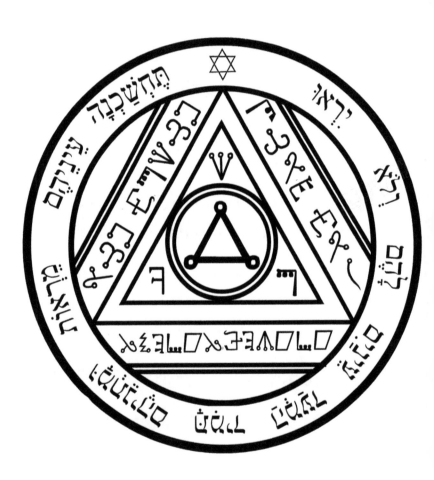

"It serveth excellently for the operation of invisibility, when correctly made."

Divine names: Shaddai.
The passing the river text is allegedly Gen 1:1 - however the text is very hard to decipher.

The versicle is from Psalms 96:24 and 135:16:

"Let their eyes be darkened that they see not and make their loins continually to shake. They have eyes and see not."

Obscurentur oculi eorum ne videant et dorsum eorum semper incurva. Oculos habent et non videbunt.

תֶּחְשַׁכְנָה עֵינֵיהֶם מֵרְאוֹת וּמָתְנֵיהֶם תָּמִיד הַמְעַד. עֵינַיִם לָהֶם וְלֹא יִרְאוּ

SEVENTH PENTACLE
OF THE SUN

"If any be by chance imprisoned or detained in fetters of iron, at the presence of this Pentacle, which should be engraved in Gold on the day and hour of the Sun, he will be immediately delivered and set at liberty."

The versicle is from Psalm 116:16,17:

"Thou hast loosed my bands. I will offer to thee the sacrifice of thanksgiving, and will call upon the name of the LORD."

Disrupisti vincula mea Tibi sacrificabo hostiam laudis et in nomine Domini invocabo

תְחַתְפ יָרֶסׄומְל,
,הְל-חַבְזֶא חַבֶז הָדׄות ; מֶׄשְׁבׄו הָוהְי אְרְקֶא

Names of the Rulers of the Elements

שרף: - Seraph

אדיאל: - Ariel

תרשיש: - Tharsis

כרוב: - Cherub

Names of the Angels of the Elements

אראל: - Arel

פורלאך: - Phorlakh

חסן: - Chasan

טל־יהד: - Taliahad

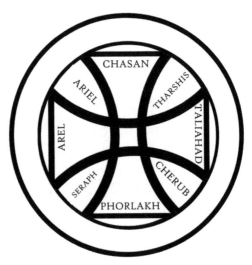

PENTACLES OF VENUS

1 = For control of the spirits of Venus
2 - For grace and honour, as well as all
things under the rule of Venus.
3 - For love
4 - Causes the spirits of venus to obey,
and to obtain whichever person
you desire
5 - For Love

Make these pentacles on a friday, out of
copper. Where copper is not availiable,
use virgin parchment and green ink.

FIRST PENTACLE
OF VENUS

"This and those following serve to control the Spirits of Venus, and especially those herein written."

Angelic Names

נעאריאל׃ Nangariel

סוכוהיה׃ Socodiah/Socohiah

אחליה׃ Acheliah

נוגהיאל׃ Nogahiel

SECOND PENTACLE OF VENUS

"These Pentacles are also proper for obtaining grace and honour, and for all things which belong unto Venus, and for accomplishing all thy desires herein."

The internal characters of this seal spell out names of the spirits of venus.

The versicle here is from The Song of Solomon 8:6

Put me as a seal upon thy heart, as a seal upon thy arm, for love is strong as death

~

pone me ut signaculum super cor tuum ut signaculum super brachium tuum quia fortis est ut mors dilectio

שִׂימֵנִי כַחוֹתָם עַל-לִבֶּךָ כַּחוֹתָם עַל-זְרוֹעֶךָ כִּי-עַזָּה כַמָּוֶת אַהֲבָה

THIRD PENTACLE
OF VENUS

"This, if it be only shown unto any person, serveth to attract love. Its Angel Monachiel should be invoked in the day and hour of Venus, at one o'clock or at eight."

The names within this pentacle are: IHVH, Adonai, Ruach, Achides, Aegalmiel, Monachiel and Degaliel

The versicle of this pentagram is from Genesis 1:28
And God blessed them, and he said "Increase and multiply, and fill the earth, and subdue it"

Benedixitque illis Deus, et ait: Crescite et multiplicamini, et replete terram, et subiicite eam

וַיְבָרֶךְ אֹתָם,אֱלֹהִים,וַיֹּאמֶר לָהֶם אֱלֹהִים פְּרוּ וּרְבוּ וּמִלְאוּ

אֶת-הָאָרֶץ, וְכִבְשֻׁהָ

FOURTH PENTACLE
OF VENUS

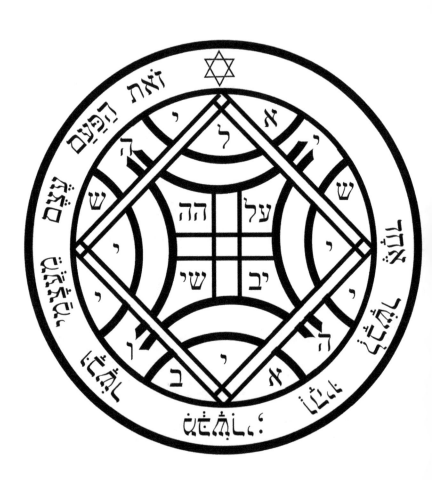

"It is of great power, since it compels the Spirits of Venus to obey, and to force on the instant any person thou wishest to come unto thee."

The versicle is Genesis 2:23,24
"This is bone of my bones, and flesh of my flesh. and they two were one flesh."

Hoc nunc, os ex ossibus meis, et caro de carne mea...et erunt duo in carne una.

זֹאת הַפַּעַם עֶצֶם מֵעֲצָמַי וּבָשָׂר מִבְּשָׂרִי וְהָיוּ לְבָשָׂר אֶחָד

DIVINE NAMES: IHVI

The other characters spell out the names of angels including: SCHII
                                                    ELI
                                                    AYIB

FIFTH PENTACLE
OF VENUS

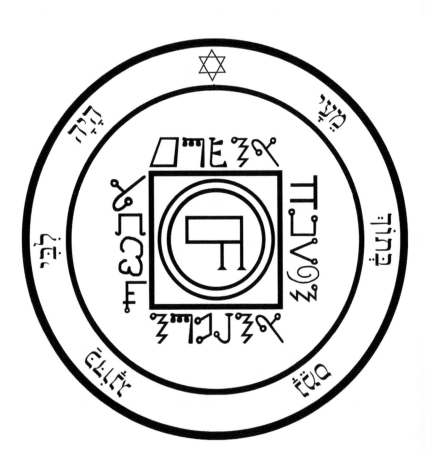

"When it is only showed unto any person soever, it inciteth and exciteth wonderfully unto love."

The characters around the central figure are in the "Passing of the River" script, but even using Mather's own tables i was unable to discipher them.

The versicle here is Psalm 22 line 15

my heart is become like wax; it is melted in mine inmost parts.

mea factum est cor meum tamquam cera liquescens in medio ventris mei

הָיָה לִבִּי, כַּדּוֹנָג; נָמֵס, בְּתוֹךְ מֵעָי.

PENTACLES OF MERCURY

1 - Invokes the spirits of the firmament
2 -For anything contrary to nature
3 - For invoking the spirits of mercury
4 -For hidden knowledge and to have
the *Allatori* perform embassies
5 - Commands the spirits of mercury
and opens doors.

Make on A Wednesday, from an alloy
metal, or using multicoloured ink on
virgin parchment.

FIRST PENTACLE
OF MERCURY

"It serveth to invoke the Spirits who are under the Firmament."

The inner characters spell out the angelic name Agiel

The characters around the outer circle spell out the angelic name Yekahel

SECOND PENTACLE
OF MERCURY

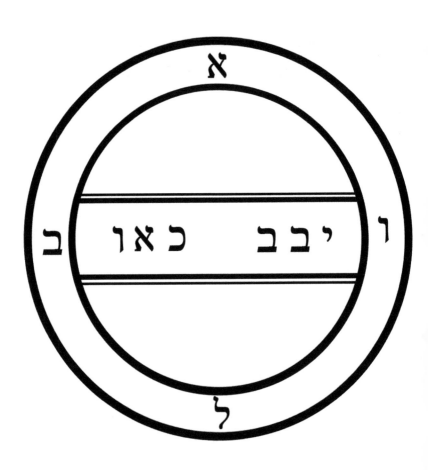

"The Spirits herein written serve to bring to effect and to grant things which are contrary unto the order of Nature; and which are not contained under any other head. They easily give answer, but they can with difficulty be seen."

The characters in this pentacle spell out the names of the following spirits:
BOEL
YBB
KhAV

THIRD PENTACLE OF MERCURY

"This and the following serve to invoke the Spirits subject unto Mercury; and especially those who are written in this Pentacle."

Names of the spirits surrounded this pentalce:

סאוניה:	Savaniah
כוכביאל:	Kokaviel
חכמהיאל:	Chokmahiel
גדוריה:	Ghedoriah

FOURTH PENTACLE
OF MERCURY

"This is further proper to acquire the understanding and Knowledge of all things created, and to seek out and penetrate into hidden things; and to command those Spirits which are called Allatori to perform embassies. They obey very readily."

The letters within the central star spell out the following "IHVH, *fix thou the volatile, and let there be unto the void restriction*"

The versciel around this pentacle reads: "Spientia *et virtus in domo ejus, et Scientia omnium rerum manet apud sum in saculum saculi*"

Wisdom and virtue are in this house and the knowledge of the all things remaineth with him forever.
Divine Names: IHVH & EL

FIFTH PENTACLE OF MERCURY

"This commandeth the Spirits of Mercury, and serveth to open doors in whatever way they may be closed, and nothing it may encounter can resist it."

Divine Names: EL AB
IHVH

The versicle is pslam 23:7

"Lift up your heads, O ye gates, and be ye lifted up, ye everlasting doors; that the King of glory may come in"

Adtollite portas principes vestras et elevamini portae aeternales et introibit rex gloriae

שְׂעָרִים,רָאשֵׁיכֶם,וְהִנָּשְׂאוּ,פִּתְחֵי עוֹלָם ;
וְיָבוֹא, מֶלֶךְ הַכָּבוֹד

PENTACLES OF THE MOON

1 - For the conjuration of lunar spirits and the opening of doors

2 - For safe travel over water and halts supernatural rain

3 - Protects those who travel by night and over water

4 - Defends against witchcraft and helps attain knowledge of herbs & stones

5 - For prophetic dreams, destruction of enemies and necromancy.

6 - Causes rain

Create these pentacles on a monday, from silver or on virgin parchement using silver ink.

FIRST PENTACLE
OF THE MOON

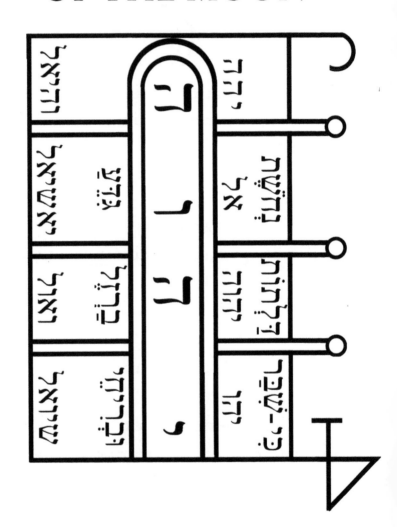

"This and the following serve to call forth and invoke the Spirits of the Moon; and it further serveth to open doors, in whatever way they may be fastened."

Divine Names	Angelic Names
IHH	Schioel
EL/AL	Vaol
IHVH	Yashiel
IHV	Vehiel

The versicle here is Psalm 107 line 16

For He hath broken the gates of brass,
And cut the bars of iron in sunder.

Quia contrivit portas aereas et vectes ferreos confregit

כִּי-שִׁבַּר,דַּלְתוֹת נְחֹשֶׁת; וּבְרִיחֵי בַרְזֶל גִּדֵּעַ

SECOND PENTACLE
OF THE MOON

"This serveth against all perils and dangers by water, and if it should chance that the Spirits of the Moon should excite and cause great rain and exceeding tempests about the Circle, in order to astonish and terrify thee; on showing unto them this Pentacle, it will all speedily cease."

The versicle here is Psalm 118 line 12

"In God do i trust, I will not be afraid; what can man do unto me?"

Dominus mihi adiutor non timebo quid faciat mihi homo

בֵּאלֹהִים בָּטַחְתִּי,לֹא אִירָא;מַה- יַּעֲשֶׂה אָדָם לִי

Divine Names: EL   אל
Angelic Name: Abariel   אבריאל

THIRD PENTACLE
OF THE MOON

This being duly borne with thee when upon a journey, if it be properly made, serveth against all attacks by night, and against every kind of danger and peril by Water.

Divine Names

AUB	VEVAPHEL
און	וואפאל

The versicle around this pentacle is from Psalm 40 Line 14

Be pleased, O LORD, to deliver me; O LORD, make haste to help me

Conplaceat tibi Domine ut eruas me
Domine ad adiuvandum me respice

רְצֵה יְהוָה, לְהַצִּילֵנִי; יְהוָה,לְעֶזְרָתִי חוּשָׁה.

FOURTH PENTACLE
OF THE MOON

"This defendeth thee from all evil sorceries, and from all injury unto soul or body. Its Angel, Sophiel, giveth the knowledge of the virtue of all herbs and stones; and unto whomsoever shall name him, he will procure the knowledge of all"

Ruled over by the angel Sophiel, who teachers the nature of herbs and stones.

The versicle here is Jeremiah 17:18

"Let them be confounded who persecute me, and let me not be confounded; let them fear, and not I"

Confundantur qui persequuntur me et non confundar ego paveant illi et non pavean ego

אהיה
אשר
אהיה

Divine Name:
Eheieh Asher Eheieh

יההאל
סופיאל

Angelic Names
Yahel and Sophiel

FIFTH PENTACLE
OF THE MOON

"It serveth to have answers in sleep. Its Angel Iachadiel serveth unto destruction and loss, as well as unto the destruction of enemies. Thou mayest also call upon him by Abdon and Dalé against all Phantoms of the night, and to summon the souls of the departed from Hades."

DIVINE NAMES		ANGELIC NAMES	
יהוה	IHVH	יכריאל	IACHADIEL
אלהים	ELOHIM	אזראל	AZAREL

The versicle is Psalm 68 line 2

"Let God arise, let His enemies be scattered; and let them that hate Him flee before Him."

Exsurgat Deus et dissipentur inimci eius et fugiant qui oderunt eum a facie eius

יָקוּם אֱלֹהִים, יָפוּצוּ אוֹיְבָיו;וְיָנוּסוּ מְשַׂנְאָיו,מִפָּנָיו.

SIXTH PENTACLE OF
THE MOON

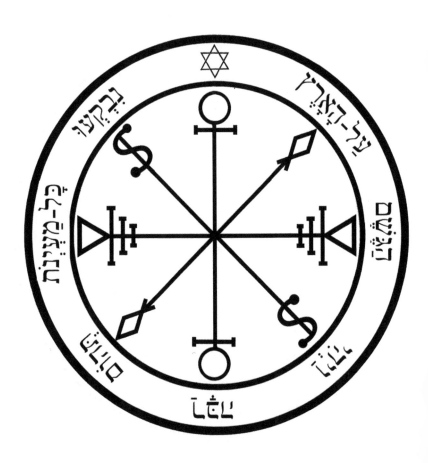

"This is wonderfully good, and serveth excellently to excite and cause heavy rains, if it be engraved upon a plate of silver; and if it be placed under water, as long as it remaineth there, there will be rain. It should be engraved, drawn, or written in the day and hour of the Moon."

The versicle around this pentacle is:
GENESIS 7:11/12
All the fountains of the great deep were broken up . . . and the rain was upon the earth.

rupti sunt omnes fontes abyssi magnæ, et facta est pluvia super terram

עַל - הָאָרֶץ הַגֶּשֶׁם וַיְהִי רַבָּה תְּהוֹם כָּל-מַעְיְנֹת נִבְקְעוּ

Lightning Source UK Ltd.
Milton Keynes UK
UKHW021628020720
365920UK00003B/383